The Clothing Store Blueprint

The Clothing Store Blueprint

Your Complete Guide to Launching, Growing, and Succeeding in your Fashion Venture

TYNESIA HALFACRE

To my cherished son, Tyreeq Halfacre,

This entire series is dedicated to you, with all my love and unwavering belief in your limitless potential. May it serve as a testament that you can achieve anything you set your mind to. As you embark on your journey through life, always remember that I will forever be there for you. When no one else is around, I will be your biggest supporter, motivator, and cheerleader.

Believe in yourself, my dear son, and never let anything or anyone hinder your path to success. You have the power to be anything you want to be and to accomplish anything you desire. Embrace every challenge as an opportunity for growth, and never shy away from chasing your dreams.
Tyreeq, you have incredible potential and boundless opportunities ahead of you. Know that I believe in you wholeheartedly, and I am here to encourage and uplift you through every triumph and challenge.

No matter where life takes you or what obstacles you encounter, I will stand by your side with unwavering support and endless love. You are capable of achieving greatness, and I will always be here to celebrate your successes and provide guidance during difficult times.

You are not alone in this journey, my dear son. Lean on me, trust in yourself, and let nothing deter you from reaching for the stars. Your dreams are within reach, and I am here to help you turn them into reality. May this eBook series remind you that I am here to support and encourage you every step of the way. Your future is bright, and I cannot wait to see you achieve greatness.

With boundless love, pride, and encouragement,

Mom

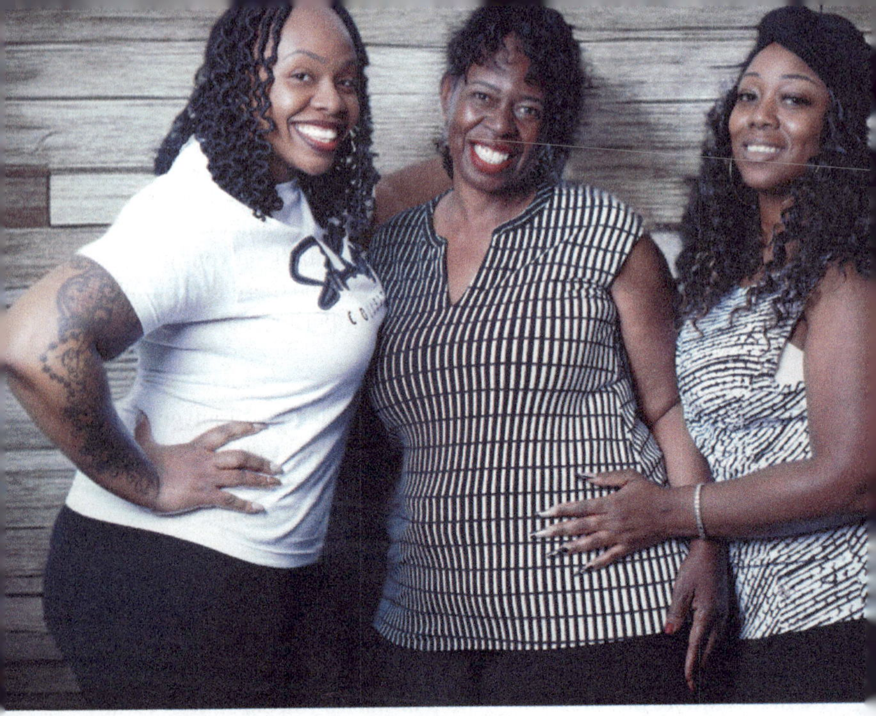

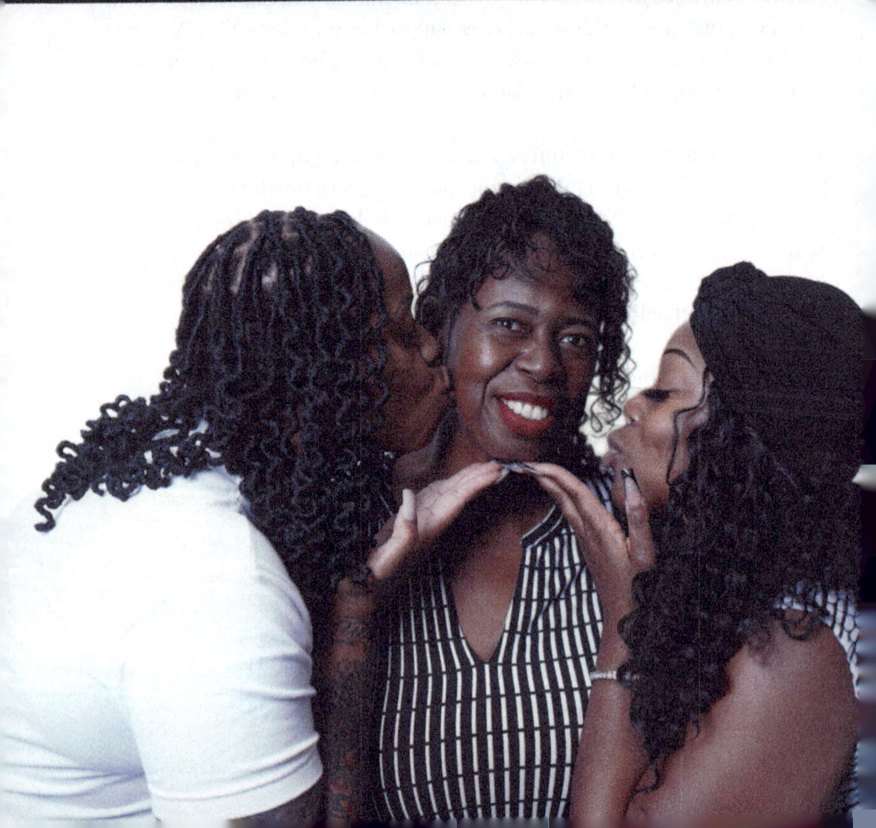

To my incredible Mom and Sister,

This entire series is also dedicated to you all, my top supporters and best friends. Your unwavering love, encouragement, and belief in me have been the foundation of all my achievements. You have stood by me through every challenge, celebrated every success, and provided the strength and motivation I needed to persevere. Together, you have both been my rock, my cheerleaders, and my confidantes. I credit the woman I am today to the remarkable love and support you both have given me.

Sister, your unwavering strength, boundless bravery, and remarkable resilience, stand as a pillar of inspiration in my life. Your courage in facing life's challenges and your ability to bounce back with grace and determination have truly taught me the true meaning of being strong. Your presence in my life is a constant reminder of the beauty of unconditional love and our unbreakable bond. I am grateful for the countless lessons you have taught me and because of you, I tackle every obstacle with confidence and determination.

Mom, your wisdom, love, and enormous heart have shaped my intelligence, personality, and passion for helping others. You have always been my guiding light, teaching me the importance of kindness, compassion, and resilience. Your unwavering faith in me has been my anchor, and I am eternally grateful for everything you have done and continue to do. Your influence has made me a better person, and I strive to emulate your grace and generosity every day. Thank you for being my heart and soul, for standing by me through every storm, and for being the reason I continue to reach for the stars.

With all my love and gratitude,

Tynesia

To Jasmine "Kookie" Daniels,

My Kookie, My Kookie, My Kookie I am also dedicating this entire series to you! Two years ago, no one could have ever convinced me that I would be an author. Honestly, I thought you lost your mind when you called me in May of 2022 and told me to write a book. You saw something in me that I NEVER saw in myself. No matter what I tried to say to push back on the idea, you weren't letting up...and for that I'm truly grateful. What I appreciate the most is that you only made that one phone call to me, you never hounded me or were overly aggressive, I guess you knew that idea had to simmer a long time inside of me lol.

Your conviction and belief in my abilities have been the guiding light that led me on this journey of authoring these books. Your infectious enthusiasm and boundless optimism inspired me to take on such a task and share my knowledge with others. Your belief in me, even when I doubted myself, has been a source of strength and motivation throughout the writing process. Several times throughout this journey, I was ready to throw in the towel, but I kept hearing you say "You HAVE to do this Ty," and I kept going.

This dedication is a token of my deepest gratitude and appreciation for your friendship, guidance, and unwavering support. Thank you for having the vision that was meant for me even when I could not see it. Your impact on my life and this project is immeasurable, and I am forever grateful for your presence in my life.

With love and gratitude,

-Ty

To Christian & Dominic of Mimi's Tacos and French Fries,

This entire series is also dedicated to you all....you all were the spark that ignited my journey into the world of commercial real estate, and for that, I am forever grateful. As the very first business to trust me with helping you locate and secure your first brick and mortar restaurant location, you not only placed your trust in me but also helped me discover my true passion and calling in the real estate industry.

Your vision, determination, and willingness to take a chance on a new commercial Realtor inspired me to pursue this path wholeheartedly. Your belief in me gave me the confidence to step outside of my comfort zone and embrace the challenges and opportunities of commercial real estate.

From our first walk through, to the successful completion of your lease agreement, every interaction with you guys has been a source of inspiration and motivation for me. Your dedication to your business and your unwavering commitment to excellence has left a permanent mark on me, shaping my approach to real estate and business relationships.

I am deeply grateful for the role you played in my journey and for the lessons I've learned from our collaboration. You helped me find my niche, my passion, and my purpose in real estate, and for that, I will always hold a special place in my heart for you all and Mimi's Tacos and French Fries.

Thank you for believing in me and for entrusting me with such an important milestone in your business journey. It has been an honor and a privilege to work with you, and I look forward to continuing to support and celebrate your success in the years to come.

With sincere gratitude,

Tynesia Halfacre

WHAT'S INSIDE

INTRODUCTION

Welcome to Your Fashion Dream!

Congratulations on taking this exciting leap into the world of retail! If you are holding this eBook, it means you are ready to turn your passion for style into something extraordinary—an actual clothing store of your own.

Imagine it: Your very own space, filled with racks of beautifully curated clothes that reflect your unique taste and style. Picture the buzz of customers, the excitement of new collections, and the satisfaction of seeing your brand come to life. This is not just about opening a store; it's about creating a destination where fashion lovers like you can connect with something special.

Maybe you have been dreaming about this for a while, sketching designs, following trends, or simply obsessing over the perfect outfit combinations. Or perhaps you are ready to launch your own line and need the right place to showcase your creations. Whatever your story, finding the perfect commercial space is a thrilling chapter in your fashion journey.

In this eBook, we are going to guide you through the exciting process of locating that ideal spot for your clothing store. From understanding your brand's identity to scouting locations and negotiating leases, we will cover everything you need to know to make this dream a reality.

But beyond the practical aspects, remember why you started. This is not just about bricks and mortar; it is about translating your love for fashion into a tangible expression of creativity and entrepreneurship. Your store will be more than just a business—it will be a reflection of your passion and a platform to share your style with the world.

So, buckle up, ignite your passion, and get ready to embark on this thrilling adventure. Let's find that perfect space together and make your fashion dream a stunning reality. The journey starts now!

By the end of this guide, you will have a clear roadmap for finding, securing, and launching your clothing store in a way that reflects your style, resonates with your audience, and sets the stage for your success in the fashion industry. Let's get started on this exciting journey together!

ARE YOU
READY?

ARE
YOU
READY?

Chapter 1: Are You Ready To Own a Clothing Store?

Congratulations on considering the leap into establishing your own clothing store! Before diving into the exciting process of finding a commercial space, let's ensure you are fully prepared for this entrepreneurial journey. In this chapter, we will explore key considerations and essential preparations to evaluate your readiness for launching a successful clothing business.

1.1 *Business Plan: Building a Solid Foundation*

One of the most critical steps before venturing into any business is crafting a comprehensive business plan. Your business plan will serve as a roadmap outlining your goals, target market, financial projections, and operational strategies. It's not just a document for investors; it's a vital tool that helps you clarify your vision and navigate challenges effectively.

Actionable Tip: Start by outlining your business's mission and vision, define your unique selling proposition (USP), and conduct thorough market research to understand your industry landscape.

1.2 *Cost: Understanding Financial Requirements*

Running a clothing store involves various costs beyond the initial investment in a commercial space. Consider expenses such as inventory procurement, utilities, employee salaries, insurance, and marketing. Understanding and budgeting for these costs upfront is crucial to avoid financial pitfalls later.

Actionable Tip: Create a detailed budget that includes startup costs and monthly operational expenses. Factor in contingencies to ensure you're financially prepared for unforeseen circumstances.

1.3 *Responsibility: Committing to Business Ownership*

Owning a business requires dedication, time, and effort. Are you ready to take on the responsibilities of managing daily operations, overseeing staff, handling customer inquiries, and adapting to market demands? It's essential to be realistic about the time and energy needed to make your clothing store thrive.

Actionable Tip: Reflect on your personal commitments and lifestyle to assess your capacity to run a business. Consider building a support network or hiring assistance to manage tasks effectively.

1.4 *Customer Service: Building Relationships*

Customer service is the cornerstone of retail success. Prepare yourself for interactions with diverse customers, ranging from enthusiastic shoppers to challenging individuals. Developing excellent communication skills and a customer-centric approach will set your store apart.

Actionable Tip: Role-play common customer scenarios to practice handling inquiries, complaints, and feedback professionally and positively.

1.5 *Business Structure: Legal Considerations*

Decide on the legal structure of your business, such as a sole proprietorship, partnership, LLC, or corporation. Each structure has unique implications for taxes, liability, and operational flexibility. Consult with a legal advisor to choose the most suitable option for your business goals.

Actionable Tip: Research the legal requirements for registering your business and obtaining necessary permits or licenses in your area.

1.6 *Policies & Procedures: Establishing Guidelines*

Establishing clear policies and procedures early on helps streamline operations and ensure consistency. Define policies for sales transactions, returns, exchanges, employee conduct, and inventory management. Consistent policies build trust and enhance the customer experience.

Actionable Tip: Document your policies and procedures in a handbook for reference by employees and customers.

1.7 *Marketing & Advertising Plan: Attracting Your Audience*

No business can thrive without effective marketing and advertising. Develop a strategic plan to promote your clothing store, leveraging social media, email marketing, partnerships, and local advertising. Identify your target audience and tailor your messaging to resonate with their preferences.

Actionable Tip: Research marketing techniques specific to retail and fashion industries, and outline a marketing calendar to stay organized and proactive.

Additional Key Points

a. Inventory Management: Explore strategies for sourcing and managing inventory to optimize stock levels and meet customer demand efficiently.

b. Technology Integration: Consider adopting retail technology tools such as POS systems, inventory management software, and e-commerce platforms to streamline operations and enhance customer experience.

By considering these essential aspects before securing a commercial space, you will be better prepared to embark on your journey as a clothing store owner. Each step is fundamental to your success and will guide your decision-making process as you progress through this exciting entrepreneurial endeavor. Stay focused, stay motivated, and let's build the foundation for your dream clothing store together!

CUSTOMER SERVICE

Chapter 2: THE POWER OF EXCEPTIONAL CUSTOMER SERVICE
Adapting a Customer Centric Mindset

Exceptional customer service is not just a component of a successful clothing store business—it is the cornerstone that supports longevity, growth, and sustainability. In this dedicated chapter, we will explore the profound impact of outstanding customer service on your business and equip you with the knowledge and skills to navigate various customer situations effectively.

2.1 *Importance of Exceptional Customer Service*

- Building Customer Loyalty: Exceptional customer service fosters trust and loyalty among your customers, encouraging repeat business and positive word-of-mouth referrals.
- Enhancing Brand Reputation: Positive customer experiences elevate your brand reputation, setting you apart from competitors and attracting new customers through glowing recommendations.
- Driving Business Growth: Satisfied customers are more likely to make additional purchases and become brand advocates, fueling business growth and profitability.

2.2 *Key Principles of Exceptional Customer Service*

- Empathy and Understanding: Develop empathy to connect with customers on a personal level and understand their needs and preferences.
- Timely and Responsive Communication: Respond promptly to customer inquiries, feedback, and complaints to demonstrate attentiveness and commitment to customer satisfaction.
- Problem-Solving Skills: Equip yourself with effective problem-solving techniques to address customer issues and resolve conflicts in a professional and satisfactory manner.

2.3 _Types of Customer Situations and How to Handle Them_

- Handling Complaints and Dissatisfaction: Learn strategies for de-escalating tense situations, empathizing with upset customers, and resolving complaints efficiently.
- Dealing with Difficult Customers: Gain insights into managing challenging customer personalities, such as aggressive or demanding individuals, while maintaining professionalism and composure.
- Managing Customer Expectations: Set clear expectations and communicate transparently to manage customer expectations effectively and prevent misunderstandings.

2.4 _Continuous Improvement and Feedback_

- Seeking Customer Feedback: Encourage customer feedback through surveys, reviews, and suggestion channels to identify areas for improvement and demonstrate a commitment to customer satisfaction.
- Employee Training and Development: Invest in ongoing training and development for staff members to enhance their customer service skills and adaptability.

Actionable Steps for Implementation

a. Establish Customer Service Standards: Define clear guidelines and standards for delivering exceptional customer service across all touch points.
b. Role-Playing Exercises: Conduct role-playing exercises to simulate various customer scenarios and practice effective communication and problem-solving techniques.
c. Celebrate Success Stories:
 Recognize and celebrate instances of exceptional customer service to inspire and motivate staff members to consistently exceed customer expectations.

By mastering the art of exceptional customer service, you will cultivate lasting relationships with customers, drive business growth, and ensure the long-term success and sustainability of your clothing store. Remember, every customer interaction is an opportunity to create a positive impact and elevate your brand reputation in the competitive fashion retail landscape. Let's prioritize outstanding customer service as the foundation of your business's success!

4

5

6

7

8

6

SALES

8

SALES
FOR
SUCCESS

Chapter 3: Sales for Success-
Mastering Sales for Your Clothing Store

In the competitive world of retail, mastering the art of sales is essential for driving revenue, attracting more customers, and achieving business growth. This chapter is dedicated to equipping you with valuable sales tips and tactics that you can apply immediately to become a better salesman and close more clients for your clothing store. Let's dive into actionable strategies and insights to elevate your sales game.

3.1 *Build Rapport and Establish Trust*

Tip: Before diving into sales pitches, focus on building rapport and establishing trust with potential customers. Show genuine interest in their needs and preferences.

Importance: Building rapport creates a positive connection, making customers more receptive to your recommendations and offers.

Implementation: Begin conversations with open-ended questions to understand customers' preferences. Listen actively and tailor your recommendations based on their responses.

3.2 *Highlight Unique Selling Proposition (USP)*

Tip: Clearly communicate your clothing store's unique selling proposition (USP)—what sets you apart from competitors. Highlight key benefits and value propositions.

Importance: A compelling USP captures attention, differentiates your brand, and convinces customers to choose your store over others.

Implementation: Craft a concise and compelling elevator pitch that articulates your store's USP. Emphasize quality, exclusivity, affordability, or any other unique aspect that resonates with your target audience.

3.3 *Overcome Objections with Confidence*

Tip: Anticipate common objections (e.g., price, fit, style) and prepare confident responses that address customers' concerns.

Importance: Overcoming objections demonstrates expertise and reassures customers, leading to increased trust and higher conversion rates.

Implementation: Role-play challenging scenarios with colleagues to practice handling objections effectively. Offer solutions and alternatives to address customers' specific concerns.

3.4 *Create a Sense of Urgency*

Tip: Use scarcity and urgency tactics (e.g., limited-time offers, exclusive collections) to create a sense of urgency and motivate customers to make purchasing decisions.

Importance: Urgency drives action and encourages customers to act quickly, reducing procrastination and increasing sales.

Implementation: Promote limited-time promotions or special discounts to incentivize immediate purchases. Clearly communicate expiration dates or limited availability to encourage prompt action.

3.5 *Follow Up and Nurture Relationships*

Tip: The fortune is in the FOLLOW-UP! Do not overlook the importance of follow-up after initial interactions. Follow up with potential customers to answer questions, provide additional information, or offer personalized recommendations.

Importance: Follow-up demonstrates dedication and commitment, fostering long-term relationships with customers and encouraging repeat business.

Implementation: Utilize customer relationship management (CRM) tools to track interactions and schedule follow-up communications. Personalize follow-up messages based on customers' preferences and previous interactions.

3.6 _Leverage Social Proof and Testimonials_

Tip: Showcase customer testimonials, reviews, and social proof (e.g., endorsements from influencers or celebrities) to build credibility and trust.
Importance: Social proof validates your brand's reputation and encourages hesitant customers to make purchasing decisions.
Implementation: Display customer testimonials on your website, social media channels, or in-store signage. Encourage satisfied customers to share their experiences and recommendations.

3.7 _Continuously Improve and Adapt_

Tip: Embrace a growth mindset and continuously seek opportunities to improve your sales techniques. Stay adaptable and open to feedback.
Importance: Continuous improvement leads to enhanced sales performance, increased customer satisfaction, and sustained business success.
Implementation: Attend sales training workshops, read sales books, and seek mentorship from experienced sales professionals. Experiment with new approaches and strategies to refine your sales skills over time.

By applying these sales tips and tactics, you will enhance your ability to attract more customers, close more deals, and drive revenue for your clothing store. Remember, successful salesmanship is a combination of skill, strategy, and genuine passion for delivering value to customers. Implement these actionable insights and watch your sales performance soar!

Here's to mastering sales and achieving unprecedented success in your clothing store business journey!

BUSINESS
ESSENTIALS

Chapter 4: Business Must-Haves:
Essentials for Running a Successful Clothing Store

Congratulations on nearing the final steps of launching your clothing store! In this crucial chapter, we will delve into all the essential elements you will need to equip your brick-and-mortar establishment for success. From equipment and furniture to staffing and partnerships, let's leave no stone unturned in preparing your business for a grand opening and sustained operations.

4.1 _Equipment and Fixtures_

- Point of Sale (POS) System: Invest in a reliable POS system for processing transactions, managing inventory, and generating sales reports. Choose a system tailored to retail needs, with features like barcode scanning and inventory tracking.
- Clothing Racks and Shelving: Select sturdy and visually appealing clothing racks, shelves, and displays to showcase your merchandise effectively.
- Fitting Rooms: Install well-lit and spacious fitting rooms with mirrors for customers to try on clothing comfortably.
- Security Systems: Implement security cameras, alarms, and anti-theft tags to protect inventory and ensure a safe shopping environment.
- Storage and Backroom Equipment: Equip your store with storage shelves, garment racks, and organizational tools for efficient inventory management.

4.2 _Furniture and Décor_
- Checkout Counter: Choose a functional and stylish checkout counter equipped with a cash register, payment terminal, and storage drawers.
- Seating Areas: Provide seating areas for customers to rest and enhance their shopping experience.
- Mirrors and Lighting: Install mirrors strategically to assist customers in trying on clothing. Optimize lighting to highlight merchandise and create an inviting ambiance.

4.3 *Staffing and Training*

- Sales Associates: Hire knowledgeable and customer-oriented sales associates to assist customers, provide styling advice, and drive sales.
- Training Programs: Implement training programs to educate staff on product knowledge, customer service, and POS system operations.

4.4 *Good Partnerships and Services*

- Wholesale Accounts: Establish relationships with wholesale suppliers or clothing brands to procure inventory at competitive prices.
- Local Vendors and Services: Partner with local vendors for services like printing (for promotional materials), cleaning, and maintenance.

4.5 *Licenses and Permits*

- Business License: Obtain a business license from the local government to legally operate your clothing store.
- Sales Tax Permit: Apply for a sales tax permit to collect and remit sales tax on merchandise sold.
- Employer Identification Number (EIN): Obtain an EIN from the IRS for tax purposes.

4.6 *Marketing and Promotion*

- Website and Online Presence: Develop a professional website and establish a presence on social media platforms to showcase your inventory and engage with customers.
- Partnerships with Influencers: Collaborate with fashion influencers or local personalities to promote your store and attract a wider audience.

4.7 *Financial Management*

- Accounting Software: Use accounting software to track expenses, manage payroll, and monitor financial performance.

- Budgeting and Cash Flow Management: Develop a budget and cash flow projections to ensure financial stability and sustainability.

Actionable Steps for Implementation

a. Create a comprehensive checklist of all required equipment, furniture, and licenses based on your business plan and store layout.

b. Research reputable suppliers and service providers to source quality equipment and establish beneficial partnerships.

c. Develop a staffing plan and recruitment strategy to hire competent and dedicated team members.

d. Prioritize customer experience and brand identity when selecting furniture, décor, and display fixtures.

e. Stay organized and proactive in obtaining necessary licenses, permits, and insurance coverage to comply with legal requirements.

By meticulously planning and acquiring these business must-haves, you will be well-prepared to open your clothing store with confidence and set the stage for long-term success. Remember, attention to detail and commitment to excellence are key to creating a thriving retail establishment. Let's turn your vision into reality and delight customers with a memorable shopping experience!

Inventor

Name : 0.5% Nacl 50 ML
Measure : box
Month : 400

te	List
3-01	balance
8-02	Dispensing-patient-out
8-03	Department of Health
15-08-05	Dispensing-patient-in
15-08-06	Dispensing-patient-out
15-08-07	Department of Health

Chapter 5: Inventory Management and Merchandising

Efficient inventory management and strategic merchandising are key components of a successful clothing store business. In this chapter, we will explore effective techniques and strategies to optimize inventory, enhance merchandising displays, and ultimately drive sales while minimizing losses.

5.1 *Stock Tracking and Organization*

- Inventory Software: Invest in inventory management software to track stock levels, monitor product performance, and automate reordering processes based on sales trends and demand forecasts.
- ABC Analysis: Categorize inventory into A, B, and C categories based on sales velocity and value. Focus on optimizing high-value items (A category) while ensuring sufficient stock of slower-moving items (C category).
- Regular Audits: Conduct regular physical inventory audits to reconcile actual stock levels with recorded inventory data, identify discrepancies, and address issues promptly.

5.2 *Seasonal Rotations and Trend Analysis*

- Seasonal Planning: Anticipate seasonal trends and adjust inventory accordingly. Plan seasonal promotions and clearance events to manage inventory turnover effectively.
- Trend Analysis: Stay abreast of fashion trends and customer preferences through market research, customer feedback, and industry insights. Align inventory assortments with current and upcoming trends to meet customer demand.

5.3 *Merchandising Strategies*

- Planogram Development: Create visual planograms to optimize store layouts and product placements. Highlight best-selling items, feature complementary products, and create attractive displays to encourage cross-selling.

- Color Blocking and Coordination: Organize merchandise by color palettes or themes to create visually appealing displays that capture customer attention and inspire outfit coordination.
- Seasonal Displays: Refresh displays regularly to showcase new arrivals, highlight seasonal collections, and create a sense of excitement and urgency among customers.

5.4 *Minimizing Overstock and Markdowns*

- Data-Driven Forecasting: Use historical sales data and market trends to forecast demand accurately. Avoid overstocking by ordering inventory based on predictive analytics and seasonal patterns.
- Markdown Strategies: Implement strategic markdowns or promotional pricing for slow-moving inventory to minimize losses and maintain healthy profit margins.

5.5 *Effective Space Utilization*

- Optimize Store Layout: Maximize floor space utilization to accommodate a variety of products while ensuring ease of navigation for customers. Create dedicated areas for new arrivals, best-sellers, and clearance items.
- Storage Solutions: Utilize efficient storage solutions such as shelving, racks, and bins to organize backstock and optimize inventory accessibility for restocking and inventory checks.

Actionable Steps for Implementation

a. Assess Current Inventory Practices: Evaluate existing inventory management processes and identify areas for improvement based on sales performance and customer feedback.

b. Invest in Inventory Management Tools: Research and invest in inventory management software or systems that align with your business needs and budget.

c. Train Staff on Merchandising Techniques: Provide training to staff on effective merchandising techniques, including product placement, visual displays, and cross-selling strategies.

d. Monitor and Adapt: Continuously monitor inventory metrics, sales data, and customer behavior to refine inventory strategies and merchandising tactics over time.

By implementing these inventory management and merchandising strategies, you will optimize inventory turnover, enhance the shopping experience, and drive sales for your clothing store. Remember to tailor these practices to align with your brand identity, target audience preferences, and overall business objectives. Let's ensure your inventory management and merchandising efforts contribute to the overall success and profitability of your clothing store business!

CHOOSING
AN AGENT

Chapter 6: Choosing an Agent:
Your Trusted Guide in Real Estate Transactions

Congratulations on taking the next step towards acquiring the perfect commercial space for your clothing store! In this chapter, we will delve into the importance of partnering with a qualified real estate agent to navigate the complexities of the real estate market and ensure a smooth and successful transaction.

6.1 _The Importance of Representation:_

Entering into a real estate transaction without professional representation is similar to venturing into uncharted territory without a map. While it may be tempting to handle negotiations and paperwork on your own, partnering with an experienced real estate agent can provide invaluable expertise, guidance, and advocacy throughout the process. An agent acts as your trusted advisor, advocating for your best interests and ensuring that your needs and objectives are met.

Actionable Tip: Prioritize finding a reputable and experienced real estate agent who specializes in commercial properties and has a track record of success in negotiating favorable deals for clients.

6.2 _Leveraging the Agent's Knowledge and Expertise:_

Real estate agents possess in-depth knowledge of the local market dynamics, trends, and property values, giving them a unique advantage in identifying and evaluating potential commercial spaces. They can provide valuable insights into neighborhood demographics, zoning regulations, and market conditions that may impact your decision-making process. By tapping into their expertise, you can make informed decisions and navigate potential pitfalls with confidence.

Actionable Tip: Take advantage of your agent's expertise by asking questions, seeking advice, and leveraging their local market knowledge to identify suitable commercial spaces that align with your business goals and budget.

6.3 _Harnessing Negotiation Skills:_

Negotiating the terms of a real estate transaction requires finesse, tact, and strategic thinking. A skilled real estate agent acts as your advocate in negotiations, leveraging their negotiation skills and market knowledge to secure favorable terms and concessions on your behalf. Whether it's negotiating lease terms, purchase price, or tenant improvements, having an experienced agent in your corner can make a significant difference in achieving a successful outcome.

Actionable Tip: Trust your agent to negotiate on your behalf, but also communicate your priorities and objectives clearly to ensure that your interests are represented effectively during the negotiation process.

6.4 _Evaluating Time in the Business:_

When selecting a real estate agent, consider their level of experience and tenure in the industry. Agents with a proven track record and extensive experience have likely encountered a wide range of scenarios and challenges, equipping them with the knowledge and skills to navigate complex transactions effectively. Look for agents who have a solid reputation, a history of successful deals, and a deep understanding of the local market dynamics.

Actionable Tip: Research prospective agents' backgrounds, credentials, and client testimonials to assess their experience and expertise in commercial real estate transactions.

6.5 _Seeking References and Recommendations:_

Before committing to work with a real estate agent, it's essential to conduct due diligence and seek references from past clients or industry professionals. Ask for referrals from trusted colleagues, friends, or family members who have had positive experiences working with commercial real estate agents. Additionally, request references from the agent and follow up with past clients to inquire about their experiences and satisfaction with the agent's services.

Actionable Tip: Don't hesitate to ask potential agents for references and follow up with past clients to gauge their satisfaction and confidence in the agent's abilities.

In conclusion, partnering with a qualified real estate agent is crucial to navigating the complexities of commercial real estate transactions and ensuring a successful outcome for your business. By leveraging their knowledge, expertise, negotiation skills, and industry connections, you will gain a competitive advantage in identifying and securing the perfect commercial space for your business. Get ready to embark on this exciting journey with the support and guidance of a trusted real estate agent by your side!

LOCATION,
LOCATION,
LOCATION!

Chapter 7: Location, Location, Location -
Finding the Perfect Spot for Your Clothing Store

Choosing the right location for your clothing store is paramount to its success. In this chapter, we will explore the significance of location and provide actionable tips on conducting market research to identify the best area for your specific business type.

7.1 *Understanding the Importance of Location*

The saying "location, location, location" rings true in retail. Your store's location can directly impact foot traffic, brand visibility, and overall customer engagement. Consider the following factors when evaluating potential locations for your clothing store:

-Parking & Accessibility: Ensure the location offers convenient parking options for customers. Easy accessibility, including proximity to public transportation, can attract more visitors to your store.

-Traffic Patterns: Study traffic patterns in different areas throughout the day. High-traffic areas near popular destinations such as shopping centers or business districts can increase exposure and potential sales.

-Foot Traffic: Evaluate pedestrian flow around potential locations. Areas with consistent foot traffic, especially during peak shopping hours, can enhance your store's visibility and customer reach.

-Visibility: Choose a location with good visibility from the street to attract passing customers. A storefront that catches the eye and showcases your merchandise can drive spontaneous visits.

-Distance from major expressway: Consider the proximity to major transportation routes like expressways or highways. Being easily accessible from major roads can broaden your customer base and draw in visitors from surrounding areas.

7.2 *Market Research and Area Selection*

Conducting thorough market research is essential to selecting the best location for your clothing store. Follow these steps to assess market demand and identify optimal areas for your business:

-Define Your Target Audience: Understand your ideal customer demographics, including age, income level, lifestyle, and shopping preferences.

-Study Local Market Trends: Research the retail landscape in potential areas. Analyze competitor locations, consumer spending patterns, and emerging fashion trends.

-Visit Potential Locations: Personally visit prospective locations during different times of the day and week. Observe the surrounding businesses, ambiance, and customer activity.

-Engage with the Community: Connect with local residents, businesses, and community organizations to gain insights into the neighborhood culture and economic climate.

-Utilize Online Tools: Leverage online resources such as demographic data, traffic maps, and commercial real estate platforms to gather quantitative data and inform your decision-making process.

Additional Considerations

a. Safety and Security: Prioritize locations with a low crime rate and adequate security measures to ensure a safe shopping environment for customers and employees.
b. Local Regulations: Familiarize yourself with zoning regulations, business permits, and licensing requirements specific to each location to avoid potential legal hurdles.

By meticulously analyzing parking availability, traffic patterns, foot traffic, visibility, and other key factors, you will be equipped to make an informed decision when selecting the optimal location for your clothing store. Remember, a strategic location can amplify your brand's visibility and contribute to the overall success of your business. Let's find the perfect spot to showcase your fashion vision and attract enthusiastic customers!

STRIP MALL
VS
STANDALONE

Chapter 8: Choosing Between Strip Malls and Standalone Buildings

Welcome to a crucial decision point in your journey to establish and manage a successful clothing store! In this chapter, we will explore the advantages and disadvantages of choosing between strip malls and standalone buildings for your clothing store. We will highlight key points to consider for each option to help you make an informed decision that aligns with your business goals and objectives.

8.1 *Choosing a Strip Mall:*

Advantages:
- Visibility: Strip malls typically offer high visibility and exposure to passing traffic, increasing the likelihood of attracting customers and generating foot traffic for your clothing store.
- Convenience: Strip malls often provide ample parking and shared amenities such as landscaping, security, and maintenance services, making them convenient options for both tenants and customers.
- Foot Traffic: Being part of a strip mall can expose your clothing store to a steady stream of foot traffic from neighboring businesses, restaurants, and retail shops, potentially increasing business opportunities.

Disadvantages:
- Limited Flexibility: Although uncommon, strip malls may have restrictions on signage, hours of operation, and use of common areas, limiting your ability to customize and differentiate your clothing store. Most times interior changes are permitted, however, exterior modifications often times require permission from the landlord/owner.
- Shared Expenses: While shared amenities can be convenient, strip mall tenants typically share the costs of common area maintenance, utilities, and property management fees, which may result in higher operating expenses.
- Noise and Competition: Sharing a space with other businesses can lead to increased noise levels and competition for customers, potentially impacting the ambiance and exclusivity of your clothing store.

Key Considerations:

a. Survey Other Owners: Talk to other tenants in the strip mall to get their insights on the landlord, property management, and overall experience of operating a business in the strip mall.

b. Ride Around the Area: Take a drive or walk around the area surrounding the strip mall to assess the neighborhood demographics, traffic patterns, and proximity to amenities and attractions.

c. Research Other Owners: Research how many other owners operate clothing stores or similar businesses in the same area as the strip mall to gauge competition and market saturation.

d. Foot Traffic and Visibility: Evaluate the amount of foot traffic in the strip mall and the visibility of your clothing store from the main street or parking lot. Consider factors such as signage opportunities and storefront visibility to attract customers.

8.2 *Choosing a Standalone Building:*

Advantages:
- Branding and Customization: Standalone buildings offer greater flexibility for branding, signage, and exterior design, allowing you to create a unique and distinctive identity for your clothing store.
- Privacy and Exclusivity: Operating in a standalone building provides privacy and exclusivity for your store, allowing you to control the ambiance, atmosphere, and guest experience without interference from neighboring businesses.
- Potential for Expansion: Standalone buildings typically offer more space and room for expansion compared to strip malls, providing opportunities for growth and diversification of services.

Disadvantages:
- Higher Costs: Standalone buildings may have higher upfront costs for purchase or lease, as well as ongoing expenses for maintenance, utilities, and property taxes.
- Maintenance Responsibility: As the sole occupant of the building, you are responsible for all maintenance and repairs, including landscaping, parking lot maintenance, and building upkeep.
- Limited Visibility: Standalone buildings may have less visibility and exposure to passing traffic compared to strip malls, requiring additional efforts and investments in marketing and advertising to attract customers.

Key Considerations for Standalone Building

a. Accessibility: Assess the accessibility of the standalone building for both customers and employees, considering factors such as parking availability, proximity to major streets, and ease of navigation.
b. Zoning and Permits: Ensure that the standalone building is zoned appropriately for your business concept and that all necessary permits and licenses are obtainable before proceeding with leasing or purchasing.
c. Infrastructure and Utilities: Evaluate the condition of the building's infrastructure, including HVAC systems, electrical wiring, and plumbing, to identify any potential maintenance or upgrade needs.
d. Market Visibility: Consider the visibility of the standalone building within the local market and its potential to attract customers based on its location, surrounding businesses, and accessibility.
e. Future Expansion: Assess the potential for future expansion or renovation of the standalone building to accommodate growth and evolving business needs, ensuring scalability and long-term viability.

In conclusion, choosing between a strip mall and a standalone building for your clothing store requires careful consideration of the advantages, disadvantages, and key factors specific to your business needs and objectives. By surveying other owners, riding around the area, researching competition and foot traffic, and evaluating signage and visibility opportunities, you will be better equipped to make an informed decision that sets the stage for success in your fashion venture. Get ready to embark on this exciting journey with confidence, armed with the knowledge and insights to choose the best location for your business!

CHAPTER

09

DUE
DILIGENCE

Chapter 9: Navigating City Regulations – Ensuring Compliance for Your Clothing Store

Welcome to the critical chapter on contacting your city or municipality to understand the specific regulations and requirements for operating your clothing store! In this section, we will explore the essential steps to take to ensure compliance with local ordinances and regulations, covering everything from zoning to necessary licenses and permits. Engaging with municipal authorities early in the process allows you to gather essential information and requirements for operating your clothing store legally. Here's what you need to consider:

9.1 *Verify No Moratorium:* Check for any zoning moratoriums or restrictions that may impact your ability to open a clothing store in your area of interest.

9.2 *Verify Zoning:* Confirm that the intended location is zoned for commercial use, particularly retail, to avoid legal complications down the line.

9.3 *Verify Business License Process:* Understand the process and documentation required to obtain a business license. This typically involves submitting an application and paying associated fees.

9.4 *Verify Required Inspections:* Determine if specific inspections, such as building, fire, or health inspections, are mandatory before opening your store to the public.

9.5 *City-Specific Requirements:* Research city-specific regulations concerning sprinkler systems, signage, hours of operation, waste disposal, and other operational aspects.

9.6 Verify Necessary Licenses and Permits: Identify and acquire any specialized licenses or permits applicable to retail businesses, such as a sales tax permit or alcohol license if selling beverages.

9.7 *Architectural Requirements*: Determine if an architect is required for the buildout or renovation of your store space, especially if structural changes are needed.

Actionable Steps for Compliance

a. Contact the City's Planning Department: Reach out to the local planning department or zoning board to inquire about specific regulations and requirements for opening a retail business.
b. Schedule Meetings or Consultations: Arrange meetings with city officials or regulatory bodies to discuss your business plans and seek guidance on compliance.
c. Obtain Written Documentation: Request written documentation outlining all necessary permits, licenses, and inspections required for your clothing store.
d. Establish Timelines and Deadlines: Understand the timelines for application submissions, approvals, and inspections to ensure you meet all regulatory deadlines.
e. Consult Legal and Construction Professionals: Seek advice from legal experts and construction professionals to navigate complex regulatory processes effectively.

Additional Considerations

a. Accessibility Compliance: Ensure your store meets accessibility standards outlined by the Americans with Disabilities Act (ADA) to accommodate customers with disabilities.

By proactively contacting the city and diligently verifying all regulatory requirements, you'll position your clothing store for legal compliance and operational success. Taking these steps early in the process will save you time, money, and potential headaches as you work towards launching your fashion business. Let's ensure your clothing store meets all necessary standards and regulations, allowing you to focus on delivering an exceptional customer experience!

ASSESSING
THE SPACE

Chapter 10: Assessing the Commercial Space - Ensuring it's the Perfect Fit for Your Clothing Store

When selecting a commercial space for your clothing store, a thorough walk-through and inspection are essential to ensure the space meets your business needs and is suitable for your operations. In this chapter, we will explore key factors to consider during the walk-through and before signing a lease, providing actionable steps and practical tips to guide you through the process.

10.1 *Check for Structural Integrity*

- Water Damage: Look for signs of water damage, such as stains on ceilings or walls, musty odors, or warped flooring. Water damage can indicate underlying issues that may require costly repairs.
- Water Heater and HVAC: Inspect the condition of the water heater and HVAC system. Ensure they are in good working order to provide comfort for customers and employees.
- Flooring: Evaluate the condition of the flooring. Determine if repairs or replacements are needed to create a clean and attractive retail environment.
- Electrical System: Test light switches, outlets, and fixtures to confirm they function correctly and meet your store's electrical needs.
- Specific Business Requirements: If your clothing store requires specific amenities such as plumbing for water fountains or snack areas, verify that these are available and operational.

10.2 *Space Requirements and Flexibility*

- Determining Space Needs: Calculate the square footage needed for retail space, fitting rooms, storage, and office areas. Ensure the layout supports efficient operations and customer flow.
- Flexibility of the Space: Consider the adaptability of the space to accommodate future expansion or layout changes based on your business growth and evolving needs.

10.3 *ADA Accessibility and Facilities*

- Bathrooms: Check if bathrooms are ADA accessible, especially if required by law based on the size and nature of your business.

10.4 *Private Inspections*

- Professional Inspections: Engage licensed plumbers, electricians, HVAC specialists, and roofers to perform comprehensive inspections. Their expertise can uncover hidden issues and ensure the space is safe and compliant.

Actionable Steps During Walk-Through

a. Take Detailed Notes: Document observations, concerns, and potential improvements needed for the space.
b. Take Measurements: Measure the dimensions of rooms, doorways, and other critical areas to plan layout and furniture placement.
c. Ask Questions: Inquire about maintenance responsibilities, lease terms, and any restrictions or allowances related to modifications or improvements.
d. Negotiate Repairs or Improvements: Use walk-through findings to discuss with your agent so they can negotiate repairs, upgrades, or lease terms before finalizing the agreement.

Additional Considerations

a. Natural Lighting: Assess the amount of natural light entering the space. Adequate lighting enhances the shopping experience and showcases merchandise effectively.
b. Ceiling Height: Consider ceiling height requirements for hanging displays or shelving units.
c. Security Measures: Evaluate existing security features such as alarm systems, cameras, and door locks to ensure the safety of your inventory and premises.

By conducting a thorough walk-through and inspection, you will gain valuable insights into the suitability of the commercial space for your clothing store. Addressing potential issues before signing the lease will help you make informed decisions and set the stage for a successful retail operation. Let's ensure your future store location aligns with your vision and business goals!

DECIPHERING
COMMERCIAL
LEASES

Chapter 11: Understanding Different Types of Commercial Leases

Welcome to an essential chapter in your journey to establish and manage a successful clothing store business! In this section, we will explore the various types of commercial leases and outline the key differences between them. Additionally, we will clarify the responsibilities of both landlords and tenants to ensure a clear understanding of each party's obligations.

11.1 *Triple Net Lease (NNN):*

A Triple Net Lease, often abbreviated as NNN, is a lease agreement in which the tenant is responsible for paying the base rent plus all expenses associated with the property, including property taxes, insurance, and maintenance costs. Under an NNN lease, the tenant assumes the majority of the financial burden for operating and maintaining the property, while the landlord typically retains ownership and control of the property's exterior elements, such as the roof, parking lots, and landscaping.

Key Differences:
- Tenant responsible for property taxes, insurance, and maintenance costs.
- Landlord typically responsible for structural repairs and maintenance of exterior areas.

11.2 *Double Net Lease (NN):*

In a Double Net Lease, or NN lease, the tenant is responsible for paying the base rent plus property taxes and insurance, while the landlord remains responsible for maintaining the structural integrity of the building, including repairs to the roof and exterior walls. Unlike a Triple Net Lease, the tenant is not responsible for additional maintenance costs under an NN lease.

Key Differences:
- Tenant responsible for property taxes and insurance.
- Landlord responsible for structural repairs and maintenance of exterior areas.

11.3 _Net Lease (Net):_

A Net Lease, known simply as a Net lease, is a lease agreement in which the tenant pays a base rent plus a portion of the property's operating expenses, such as property taxes, insurance, and maintenance costs. The exact breakdown of expenses and responsibilities may vary depending on the specific terms negotiated between the landlord and tenant.

Key Differences:
- Tenant pays base rent plus a portion of operating expenses.
- Landlord may retain responsibility for certain maintenance and repair costs.

11.4 _Gross Lease:_
In a Gross Lease, the tenant pays a fixed monthly rent, and the landlord assumes responsibility for all operating expenses, including property taxes, insurance, maintenance, and sometimes utilities. Gross leases provide tenants with a predictable monthly rent payment, as they are not responsible for additional expenses beyond the agreed-upon rent amount.

Key Differences:
- Tenant pays fixed monthly rent.
- Landlord responsible for all operating expenses, including maintenance and utilities.

11.5 _Modified Gross Lease:_

A Modified Gross Lease combines elements of both a Gross Lease and a Net Lease, allowing for flexibility in allocating responsibilities between the landlord and tenant. Under a Modified Gross Lease, the base rent may include certain operating expenses, while the tenant may be responsible for additional expenses such as utilities or janitorial services.

Key Differences:
- Base rent may include certain operating expenses.
- Tenant may be responsible for additional expenses beyond the base rent.

11.6 _Landlord vs. Tenant Responsibilities:_

Landlords typically handle exterior maintenance and repairs, including structural elements such as the roof, exterior walls, parking lots, and landscaping. They are also responsible for property taxes, insurance, and overall property management.

Tenants are generally responsible for interior maintenance and repairs, including HVAC systems, plumbing, electrical systems, windows, and interior fixtures and finishes. They may also be responsible for utilities, janitorial services, and obtaining insurance coverage for their business operations.

Actionable Tip: Before signing a lease agreement, carefully review the terms and responsibilities outlined in the lease agreement, and seek clarification on any areas of ambiguity or concern. Consider consulting with a real estate attorney or lease advisor to ensure that the lease terms align with your business needs and objectives.

In conclusion, understanding the different types of commercial leases and the responsibilities of landlords and tenants is crucial for negotiating favorable lease terms and ensuring a successful and mutually beneficial relationship. By familiarizing yourself with the nuances of each lease type and clarifying expectations upfront, you will be better equipped to make informed decisions and protect your interests as you establish and manage your clothing store business. Get ready to embark on this journey with confidence, armed with the knowledge and understanding to navigate commercial leases effectively!

CHOOSING
THE RIGHT
CONTRACTOR

Chapter 12: Choosing the Right Contractor: Building Your Dream Team

Selecting the right contractor is critical when renovating or building out a commercial space for your clothing store. In this chapter, we will explore the importance of choosing a reputable contractor and provide actionable steps to help you make an informed decision. A reliable contractor can make a significant difference in the quality and timely completion of your store's buildout. Here's why it's crucial to select the right contractor:

12.1 *Quality of Workmanship:*
 A skilled contractor delivers high-quality workmanship, ensuring that your store reflects your brand's image and meets your expectations.
- Timely Completion: An experienced contractor adheres to timelines and project schedules, allowing you to open your store on schedule and minimize downtime.
- Compliance and Safety: Licensed contractors adhere to building codes and safety regulations, mitigating risks and ensuring compliance with legal requirements.

Actionable Steps When Choosing a Contractor

a. Verify Licensing and Bonding:
- City License: Ensure the contractor is licensed to operate in the city where your clothing store will be located. Verify their credentials with the local licensing board.
- Bonded Contractor: Choose a bonded contractor to provide financial security in case of project delays, non-completion, or disputes.
b. Request Lien Waivers:
- Protection Against Liens: Obtain lien waivers from the contractor and subcontractors to protect against potential claims on the property due to unpaid bills.
c. Review Work Samples and References:
- Portfolio: Ask for samples or photos of the contractor's previous work related to retail or commercial projects. Evaluate their style, craftsmanship, and attention to detail.
- References: Request references from past clients and contact them to inquire about their experience working with the contractor.

d. Assess Professionalism and Communication:
- Punctuality: Pay attention to the contractor's punctuality and reliability during initial meetings. Timeliness reflects professionalism and commitment.
- Communication Skills: Evaluate the contractor's communication style and responsiveness. Clear and open communication is essential for a successful partnership.

Additional Considerations

a. Insurance Coverage: Ensure the contractor carries adequate insurance coverage, including liability insurance and worker's compensation, to protect against unforeseen incidents.
b. Contract Terms: Review contract terms carefully, including project scope, timelines, payment schedules, and warranties. Seek clarification on any unclear provisions before signing.
c. Budget and Cost Estimates: Obtain detailed cost estimates and compare them with your budget to avoid unexpected expenses during the project.
d. Compatibility and Collaboration: Choose a contractor who understands your vision and is willing to collaborate to achieve your desired outcome for the clothing store.

Actionable Tips During the Selection Process

a. Request multiple bids from different contractors to compare services and pricing.
b. Conduct interviews to assess compatibility and ensure a good working relationship.
c. Trust your instincts and choose a contractor you feel comfortable and confident working with.

By following these actionable steps and considerations, you will be well-equipped to choose a reliable contractor who can bring your clothing store vision to life efficiently and professionally. Let's build a strong partnership with a contractor who shares your commitment to excellence and success!

MARKETING
&
PROMOTION

Chapter 13: Marketing and Promotion Strategies

Marketing and promotion are essential elements of building a successful clothing store business. In this chapter, we will explore a variety of strategies tailored to the industry that will help you attract customers, increase brand awareness, and ultimately drive sales.

13.1 *Digital Marketing*

- E-Commerce Website: Develop a user-friendly e-commerce website where customers can browse and purchase your clothing online. Optimize the website for mobile devices to enhance accessibility.
- Search Engine Optimization (SEO): Implement SEO techniques to improve your website's visibility on search engines like Google. Focus on relevant keywords related to your clothing niche.
- Email Marketing: Build an email list of customers and prospects to send targeted promotions, new arrivals, and exclusive offers. Personalize content to increase engagement.

13.2 *Social Media Engagement*

- Platform Selection: Identify the social media platforms where your target audience is most active (e.g., Instagram, Facebook, TikTok) and create engaging content to showcase your products.
- Influencer Partnerships: Collaborate with fashion influencers or micro-influencers to reach a wider audience and leverage their credibility to promote your brand.
- User-Generated Content: Encourage customers to share photos of themselves wearing your clothing by creating branded hashtags and offering incentives. Repost user-generated content to build community and trust.

13.3 *Local Advertising*

- Google My Business: Claim and optimize your Google My Business listing to improve local search visibility and attract nearby customers.
- Local Publications: Advertise in local newspapers, magazines, or community newsletters to reach local audiences.
- Collaborate with Local Businesses: Partner with complementary local businesses (e.g., shoe stores, salons) for cross-promotions or joint events.

13.4 _Events and Promotions_

- Pop-Up Shops: Host pop-up events or temporary installations in high-traffic areas to introduce your brand to new customers and generate buzz.
- Launch Parties: Organize a grand opening or launch party to attract media attention, influencers, and local VIPs.
- Seasonal Sales and Promotions: Offer seasonal promotions, flash sales, or bundle deals to create urgency and drive sales.

13.5 _Partnerships and Collaborations_

- Brand Collaborations: Collaborate with other brands or designers for limited-edition collections or co-branded products.
- Nonprofit Partnerships: Align with nonprofit organizations or local charities for cause-related marketing initiatives that resonate with your target audience.

Actionable Steps for Implementation

a. Develop a Marketing Plan: Outline specific goals, target audience demographics, and strategies for each marketing channel (digital, social media, local advertising).
b. Allocate Budget and Resources: Allocate a budget for marketing initiatives and consider outsourcing tasks like graphic design or social media management if needed.
c. Monitor and Analyze Performance: Use analytics tools to track the performance of your marketing campaigns. Adjust strategies based on data insights to optimize results.
d. Engage with Customers: Foster genuine relationships with customers through personalized interactions, responding to comments, and addressing feedback promptly.

c. Stay Creative and Adaptive: Experiment with new marketing ideas and stay updated on industry trends to stay ahead of competitors and capture market attention.

By implementing these marketing and promotion strategies effectively, you will elevate your clothing store's visibility, attract a loyal customer base, and ultimately drive revenue growth. Remember to tailor your approach based on your unique brand identity and customer preferences to achieve sustainable success in the competitive retail landscape. Let's ignite excitement around your clothing store and create lasting connections with fashion enthusiasts!

FINANCIAL
MANAGEMENT

Chapter 14: Financial Management for Your Clothing Store

Financial planning and budgeting are essential aspects of running a successful clothing store business. In this chapter, we will explore actionable steps to effectively manage expenses, optimize cash flow, and ensure the financial health and sustainability of your clothing store. Let's dive into key strategies for financial planning and budgeting that will set your business up for long-term success.

14.1 *Establishing a Budget*

- Startup Costs: Identify and estimate one-time startup costs, including upfront rent, renovations, inventory, equipment, and licensing fees. Allocate sufficient funds to cover these expenses before opening your store.
- Operating Expenses: Create a detailed budget for ongoing operating expenses
such as rent, utilities, payroll, marketing, insurance, and inventory replenishment. Monitor and adjust expenses regularly to maintain profitability.

14.2 *Expense Management Techniques*

- Prioritize Essential Expenses: Distinguish between essential and non-essential expenses to allocate resources effectively. Focus on investments that directly contribute to business growth and customer satisfaction.
- Negotiate Vendor Contracts: Negotiate favorable terms with suppliers and vendors to secure competitive pricing and payment terms, reducing costs and improving cash flow.

14.3 *Cash Flow Optimization*

- Monitor Cash Flow: Implement cash flow forecasting to anticipate revenue and expenses. Maintain adequate cash reserves to cover operational costs during slow periods or unexpected circumstances.
- Inventory Management: Optimize inventory turnover to reduce carrying costs and minimize excess inventory. Implement strategies to improve inventory efficiency and avoid stockouts.

14.4 _Financial Forecasting and Performance Monitoring_

- Create Financial Projections: Develop realistic financial projections based on market research, sales forecasts, and industry trends. Regularly update forecasts to reflect actual performance and adjust strategies accordingly.
- Key Performance Indicators (KPIs): Monitor financial KPIs such as gross profit margin, inventory turnover ratio, and return on investment (ROI) to assess business performance and identify areas for improvement.

14.5. _Risk Management and Contingency Planning_

- Emergency Fund: Set aside funds for unforeseen expenses or emergencies to mitigate financial risks and ensure business continuity.
- Insurance Coverage: Obtain adequate insurance coverage (e.g., liability insurance, property insurance) to protect against potential losses due to accidents, theft, or lawsuits.

Actionable Steps for Implementation

a. Create a Comprehensive Budget: Develop a detailed budget that accounts for both startup and ongoing operational expenses. Use budgeting tools or software to track expenditures and stay within budgetary limits.
b. Monitor and Control Expenses: Regularly review expenses and identify areas where costs can be reduced or optimized. Implement cost-saving initiatives without compromising quality or customer experience.
c. Seek Professional Advice: Consult with financial advisors or accountants to gain insights into financial planning strategies and ensure compliance with tax regulations and reporting requirements.
d. Plan for Growth and Expansion: Incorporate financial planning for future growth and expansion initiatives into your budget. Allocate resources for marketing campaigns, store renovations, or new product launches.

By implementing effective financial planning and budgeting strategies, you will optimize resource allocation, maintain financial stability, and position your clothing store for sustainable growth and profitability. Remember, proactive financial management is crucial to navigating challenges and seizing opportunities in the dynamic retail industry. Let's ensure your business achieves long-term financial health and success!

CUSTOMER REVIEW

CUSTOMER
EXPERIENCE

Chapter 15: Customer Experience and Satisfaction

Creating an exceptional customer experience is paramount to the success of your clothing store. In this chapter, we will explore strategies for delivering outstanding customer service, building customer loyalty, and leveraging feedback to enhance the overall shopping experience.

15.1 *Delivering Exceptional Customer Service*

- Personalized Interactions: Train your staff to engage with customers on a personal level, offering assistance, product recommendations, and styling advice based on individual preferences.
- Responsive Communication: Respond promptly to customer inquiries, feedback, and complaints across all communication channels (in-store, phone, email, social media) to demonstrate attentiveness and commitment to customer satisfaction.
- Seamless Checkout Experience: Streamline the checkout process to minimize waiting times and offer multiple payment options for convenience.

15.2 *Building Customer Loyalty Programs*

- Reward Programs: Implement a loyalty program that rewards repeat customers with discounts, exclusive offers, birthday treats, or points redeemable for future purchases.
- VIP Clubs: Create a VIP club for loyal customers, offering early access to sales, special events, and personalized perks to foster a sense of exclusivity and appreciation.

15.3 *Leveraging Customer Feedback*

- Feedback Collection: Actively seek feedback from customers through surveys, reviews, and suggestion boxes to gain insights into their experiences and identify areas for improvement.
- Implementing Improvements: Use customer feedback to make informed decisions and implement changes that enhance the overall shopping experience, such as adjusting product assortments, improving store layout, or refining customer service protocols.

15.4 _Recruiting, Training, and Retaining Talented Staff_

Recruiting, training, and retaining skilled staff members who embody your brand's values is crucial to delivering exceptional customer service and maintaining a positive work environment. Here are best practices:

- Recruitment: Seek candidates who demonstrate a passion for fashion, excellent interpersonal skills, and a customer-centric mindset during the hiring process.
- Training Programs: Develop comprehensive training programs to educate staff on product knowledge, customer service standards, and company policies. Provide ongoing training to keep skills updated.
- Empowerment and Recognition: Empower employees to make decisions that prioritize customer satisfaction. Recognize and reward outstanding performance to boost morale and foster loyalty among staff.

Actionable Steps for Implementation

a. Define Customer Service Standards: Establish clear guidelines and standards for customer interactions, ensuring consistency across all staff members.
b. Invest in Staff Development: Allocate resources to staff training and development initiatives to cultivate a skilled and knowledgeable workforce.
c. Encourage Employee Engagement: Foster a positive work culture that values employee input and encourages teamwork and collaboration.
d. Monitor Customer Satisfaction Metrics: Regularly measure customer satisfaction metrics (e.g., Net Promoter Score, customer reviews) to track performance and identify areas for improvement.

By prioritizing exceptional customer service, implementing customer loyalty programs, and investing in staff development, you will cultivate a loyal customer base and differentiate your clothing store in a competitive market. Remember, happy customers and dedicated staff are the foundation of a successful retail business. Let's elevate the customer experience and build lasting relationships with fashion enthusiasts!

RESILIENCE
PLANNING

Chapter 16: Crisis Management and Contingency Planning

In the unpredictable landscape of retail business, crisis management and adaptability are essential skills for ensuring the long-term success and resilience of your clothing store. This chapter will explore strategies for navigating unforeseen challenges, such as economic downturns, supply chain disruptions, or public health crises, while maintaining business resilience. Furthermore we will cover actionable steps to equip you with the tools to overcome adversity and thrive in the face of uncertainty.

16.1 *Develop a Crisis Management Plan*

- Risk Assessment: Conduct a comprehensive risk assessment to identify potential threats and vulnerabilities to your clothing store, such as economic fluctuations, supplier issues, or exterior crises.
- Emergency Response Protocol: Establish clear protocols and procedures for responding to crises, including communication strategies, resource allocation, and decision-making processes.
- Cross-Functional Team: Assemble a cross-functional crisis management team comprising key stakeholders and department heads to collaborate on crisis response and decision-making.

16.2 *Build Resilience Through Financial Planning*

- Maintain Financial Flexibility: Maintain healthy cash reserves and explore financial instruments (e.g., lines of credit, loans) to provide liquidity during challenging times.
- Diversify Suppliers: Reduce reliance on a single supplier by diversifying your supply chain to mitigate risks associated with supplier disruptions or shortages.

16.3 *Enhance Operational Agility*

- Adaptability in Inventory Management: Develop contingency plans for inventory management, such as alternative sourcing or adjusting product assortments based on changing market demands.
- Flexible Staffing Policies: Implement flexible staffing policies, such as cross-training employees or hiring temporary workers during peak periods, to optimize resource allocation.

16.4 *Communication and Investor Engagement*

- Transparent Communication: Maintain open and transparent communication with employees, customers, suppliers, and other stakeholders during crises. Provide regular updates and address concerns promptly.
- Customer Retention Strategies: Implement customer retention strategies, such as loyalty programs or special promotions, to maintain customer loyalty and mitigate revenue loss during challenging times.

16.5 *Learn from Past Crises and Continuous Improvement*

- Post-Crisis Evaluation: Conduct a thorough evaluation after each crisis to identify lessons learned, strengths, and areas for improvement in your crisis management approach.
- Scenario Planning: Develop scenario-based contingency plans for various crisis scenarios to enhance preparedness and responsiveness in future crises.

Actionable Steps for Implementation

a. Develop a Crisis Response Playbook: Create a comprehensive crisis response playbook outlining roles, responsibilities, and protocols for different crisis scenarios.
b. Engage in Stakeholder Collaboration: Foster collaborative relationships with suppliers, industry peers, and local community networks to share resources and support during crises.
c. Stay Informed and Proactive: Stay updated on industry trends, economic indicators, and global events that may impact your business. Proactively adapt strategies based on emerging challenges and opportunities.
d. Invest in Technology and Innovation: Leverage technology and innovation to enhance operational efficiency, automate processes, and facilitate remote work capabilities during crises.

By implementing these crisis management and adaptability strategies, you'll strengthen the resilience of your clothing store and position it to navigate challenges effectively while maintaining business continuity. Remember, adaptability and proactive planning are key to thriving in a dynamic and ever-changing business environment. Let's build a resilient foundation for your clothing store's success!

GROWTH
STRATEGIES

Chapter 17: Growth and Expansion

Scaling and expanding your clothing store operations is an exciting milestone that requires careful consideration and strategic planning. In this chapter, we will explore key considerations and strategies for scaling your business, expanding into new locations, and diversifying product offerings to fuel growth. Additionally, we will reflect on lessons learned and explore future trends in the fashion retail landscape.

17.1 *Considerations for Scaling Your Business*

- Assess Market Demand: Conduct market research to identify opportunities for expansion and assess customer demand in potential new markets.
- Evaluate Operational Capacity: Ensure your existing operations are efficient and scalable to support growth. Invest in infrastructure, technology, and staffing to accommodate increased demand.

17.2 *Strategies for Expansion*

- Franchise or Licensing: Explore franchising or licensing opportunities to expand your brand presence and reach new markets with lower financial risk.
- Open New Locations: Identify strategic locations for new stores based on demographic data, foot traffic, and competition analysis. Consider factors such as lease terms and market saturation.
- Diversify Product Offerings: Introduce complementary product lines or expand into related categories (e.g., accessories, footwear) to appeal to a broader customer base and increase sales potential.

17.3 *Reflection and Future Trends*

- Lessons Learned: Reflect on challenges, successes, and lessons learned from establishing and growing your clothing store. Identify strengths to leverage and areas for improvement.
- Future Trends and Opportunities: Stay informed about emerging trends in the fashion industry, such as sustainability, technology integration, and changing consumer behaviors. Adapt strategies to align with evolving market demands.

17.4 *Importance of Integrating Online and Offline Channels*

- Omnichannel Approach: Highlight the importance of integrating online and offline channels to provide a seamless shopping experience for customers. Implement e-commerce integration, omnichannel marketing strategies, and leverage technology (e.g., POS systems, inventory management software) to enhance customer engagement and satisfaction.

Actionable Steps for Implementation

a. Develop a Growth Plan: Create a comprehensive growth plan outlining specific objectives, timelines, and resource requirements for scaling and expansion initiatives.

b. Invest in Marketing and Branding: Allocate resources to marketing campaigns and brand-building activities to increase brand visibility and attract new customers.

c. Explore Strategic Partnerships: Collaborate with industry partners, influencers, or complementary businesses to leverage shared resources and expand market reach.

d. Monitor Performance Metrics: Establish key performance indicators (KPIs) to track progress and evaluate the success of scaling and expansion efforts. Adjust strategies based on performance data and market feedback.

By implementing thoughtful strategies for scaling and expansion, reflecting on lessons learned, and embracing future trends, you will position your clothing store for sustained growth and success in the dynamic fashion retail landscape. Remember, adaptability and innovation are essential for thriving in an evolving market. Let's chart a course for scalable growth and exciting opportunities ahead!

CONCLUSION

FINAL THOUGHTS

Conclusion - Your Path to Success in the Clothing Store Business

Congratulations! You have completed this comprehensive guide to establishing and managing a successful clothing store business! Throughout this guide, we have covered essential aspects ranging from finding the perfect commercial space and inventory management to customer experience, crisis management, and scaling your operations. By absorbing the insights, practical tips, and actionable steps provided in these chapters, you are now equipped with the knowledge and confidence to embark on this exciting entrepreneurial journey.

Reflecting on the key takeaways from our discussions, let's summarize the essential points and provide you with a quick guide checklist to reference as you navigate through the process of establishing and managing your clothing store:

Quick Guide Checklist:

1. **Business Planning**:
   - Develop a comprehensive business plan outlining your goals, target audience, competitive landscape, and financial projections.

2. **Commercial Space Selection**:
   - Consider location, accessibility, foot traffic, and lease terms when choosing the perfect space for your clothing store.

3. **Inventory Management**:
   - Implement effective stock tracking, seasonal rotations, and merchandising strategies to optimize sales and minimize losses.

4. **Customer Experience and Retention**:
   - Prioritize exceptional customer service, loyalty programs, and feedback management to enhance the overall shopping experience.

5. **Financial Planning and Budgeting**:
   - Create a detailed budget, manage expenses efficiently, and optimize cash flow to ensure financial health and sustainability.

6. **Crisis Management and Adaptability**:
   - Develop a crisis management plan, build resilience through financial planning, and stay adaptable in response to unforeseen challenges.

7. **Scaling and Expansion**:
 - Evaluate market demand, explore expansion strategies (e.g., new locations, product diversification), and embrace future trends for sustainable growth.

By following these steps and leveraging the knowledge gained from this guide, you are well-prepared to navigate the complexities of starting and managing a clothing store business. Remember, entrepreneurship is a journey filled with learning experiences and opportunities for growth. Stay proactive, adaptable, and passionate about your vision.

As you embark on this exciting venture, keep this guide handy as a valuable resource to refer back to whenever you encounter challenges or seek inspiration. Your dedication, creativity, and determination will be the driving forces behind your success in the fashion retail industry.

Believe in yourself and your vision. You have what it takes to build a thriving clothing store business that resonates with customers and contributes to the vibrant world of fashion. Embrace the journey ahead with enthusiasm and confidence, and let this guide be your trusted companion along the way.

Wishing you the best of luck in your entrepreneurial endeavors. Here's to a successful and fulfilling journey as a clothing store owner!

With this conclusion, we aim to inspire and empower you to pursue your dreams of owning and managing a successful clothing store business. Trust in your abilities, apply the knowledge gained, and continue to evolve and adapt as you build your brand in the dynamic fashion industry. The future is bright—go forth and make your mark!

Cheers,

Negotiation Bae

About the Author

Tynesia Halfacre is a dynamic entrepreneur, licensed Commercial Realtor, and certified Real Estate Negotiations Expert known in the industry as "Negotiation Bae." With a passion for entrepreneurship and a dedication to helping others achieve their goals, Tynesia has made a significant impact in the world of real estate and small business ownership in Illinois.

As a mother of one 14 year old son who is also an entrepreneur of a successful lemonade business, Tynesia understands the challenges and rewards of building a business from the ground up. Her entrepreneurial spirit and commitment to excellence have driven her to excel in her own ventures and empower others to do the same.

Helping a diverse portfolio of businesses successfully locate and secure their brick and mortar locations, Tynesia has earned a reputation for her expertise in real estate negotiation and strategic business placement. Her experience as a licensed Commercial Realtor and her commitment to client satisfaction has made her a trusted advisor and advocate for entrepreneurs seeking to establish their presence in the marketplace.

In addition to her accomplishments in real estate, Tynesia has also coached numerous entrepreneurs on best business practices, startup strategies, and the journey of entrepreneurship. Her genuine passion for helping others succeed shines through in her coaching and mentorship, inspiring individuals to dream big and take bold action towards their goals.

Through her dedication to entrepreneurship, her expertise in commercial real estate, and her commitment to empowering others, Tynesia Halfacre continues to make a positive impact on the lives and businesses of those she serves. Her story serves as a testament to the power of perseverance, passion, and the pursuit of excellence in achieving success in both business and life.

Made in the USA
Las Vegas, NV
24 September 2024

95739106R00049